THIS BOOK BELONGS TO

_____   &   _____

SHARING ADVENTURES MEANS ENJOYING THEM
100% MORE."

ADVENTURE
#07:

.... THOUGHT OF THIS.

THIS IS ON OUR BUCKET LIST BECAUSE:

....

....

....

....

PLANS AND PREPARATIONS TO MAKE THIS HAPPEN:

....

....

....

....

WE DID IT!

WHEN? .... WHERE? ....

THE STORY OF OUR ADVENTURE:

....

....

....

....

....

HIS BEST MEMORY: ( )

....

HIS BEST MEMORY: ( )

....

....

ADVENTURE
#11 :

_____ THOUGHT OF THIS.

THIS IS ON OUR BUCKET LIST BECAUSE:

_____

_____

_____

_____

PLANS AND PREPARATIONS TO MAKE THIS HAPPEN:

_____

_____

_____

_____

WE DID IT!

WHEN? _____ WHERE? _____

THE STORY OF OUR ADVENTURE:

_____

_____

_____

_____

_____

HIS BEST MEMORY: (   )

_____

HIS BEST MEMORY: (   )

_____

_____

ADVENTURE
#12:

.... THOUGHT OF THIS.

THIS IS ON OUR BUCKET LIST BECAUSE:

PLANS AND PREPARATIONS TO MAKE THIS HAPPEN:

WE DID IT!

WHEN? .... WHERE? ....

THE STORY OF OUR ADVENTURE:

HIS BEST MEMORY: ( )

HIS BEST MEMORY: ( )

ADVENTURE
13:

_____ THOUGHT OF THIS.

THIS IS ON OUR BUCKET LIST BECAUSE:

_____

_____

_____

PLANS AND PREPARATIONS TO MAKE THIS HAPPEN:

_____

_____

_____

=== WE DID IT! ===

WHEN? _____ WHERE? _____

THE STORY OF OUR ADVENTURE:

_____

_____

_____

_____

HIS BEST MEMORY: ( )

_____

HIS BEST MEMORY: ( )

_____

ADVENTURE
#14:

.... THOUGHT OF THIS.

THIS IS ON OUR BUCKET LIST BECAUSE:

....

....

....

PLANS AND PREPARATIONS TO MAKE THIS HAPPEN:

....

....

....

WE DID IT!

WHEN? .... WHERE? ....

THE STORY OF OUR ADVENTURE:

....

....

....

....

....

HIS BEST MEMORY: (   )

....

HIS BEST MEMORY: (   )

....

....

#15:

.... THOUGHT OF THIS.

THIS IS ON OUR BUCKET LIST BECAUSE:

....

....

....

PLANS AND PREPARATIONS TO MAKE THIS HAPPEN:

....

....

....

WE DID IT!

WHEN? .... WHERE? ....

THE STORY OF OUR ADVENTURE:

....

....

....

....

HIS BEST MEMORY: ( )

....

HIS BEST MEMORY: ( )

....

....

#16:

.... THOUGHT OF THIS.

THIS IS ON OUR BUCKET LIST BECAUSE:

....

....

....

PLANS AND PREPARATIONS TO MAKE THIS HAPPEN:

....

....

....

WE DID IT!

WHEN? .... WHERE? ....

THE STORY OF OUR ADVENTURE:

....

....

....

....

....

HIS BEST MEMORY: ( )

....

HIS BEST MEMORY: ( )

....

....

ADVENTURE
#17:

.... THOUGHT OF THIS.

THIS IS ON OUR BUCKET LIST BECAUSE:

....

....

....

PLANS AND PREPARATIONS TO MAKE THIS HAPPEN:

....

....

....

WE DID IT!

WHEN? .... WHERE? ....

THE STORY OF OUR ADVENTURE:

....

....

....

....

HIS BEST MEMORY: (   )

....

HIS BEST MEMORY: (   )

....

....

ADVENTURE
18 :

.... THOUGHT OF THIS.

THIS IS ON OUR BUCKET LIST BECAUSE:

....
....
....

PLANS AND PREPARATIONS TO MAKE THIS HAPPEN:

....
....
....

WE DID IT!

WHEN? .... WHERE? ....

THE STORY OF OUR ADVENTURE:

....
....
....
....
....

HIS BEST MEMORY: (   )

....

HIS BEST MEMORY: (   )

....

ADVENTURE
#19:

.... THOUGHT OF THIS.

THIS IS ON OUR BUCKET LIST BECAUSE:

....

....

....

PLANS AND PREPARATIONS TO MAKE THIS HAPPEN:

....

....

....

WE DID IT!

WHEN? .... WHERE? ....

THE STORY OF OUR ADVENTURE:

....

....

....

....

HIS BEST MEMORY: ( )

....

HIS BEST MEMORY: ( )

....

....

ADVENTURE
#20:

_____ THOUGHT OF THIS.

THIS IS ON OUR BUCKET LIST BECAUSE:

_____

_____

_____

PLANS AND PREPARATIONS TO MAKE THIS HAPPEN:

_____

_____

_____

WE DID IT!

WHEN? _____ WHERE? _____

THE STORY OF OUR ADVENTURE:

_____

_____

_____

_____

HIS BEST MEMORY: ( )

_____

HIS BEST MEMORY: ( )

_____

ADVENTURE
#21:

.... THOUGHT OF THIS.

THIS IS ON OUR BUCKET LIST BECAUSE:

PLANS AND PREPARATIONS TO MAKE THIS HAPPEN:

WE DID IT!

WHEN? .... WHERE? ....

THE STORY OF OUR ADVENTURE:

HIS BEST MEMORY: (   )   .

HIS BEST MEMORY: (   )

ADVENTURE
#22:

.... THOUGHT OF THIS.

THIS IS ON OUR BUCKET LIST BECAUSE:

....

....

....

PLANS AND PREPARATIONS TO MAKE THIS HAPPEN:

....

....

....

....

WE DID IT!

WHEN? .... WHERE? ....

THE STORY OF OUR ADVENTURE:

....

....

....

....

....

HIS BEST MEMORY: (   )

....

HIS BEST MEMORY: (   )

....

....

ADVENTURE
23:

_____ THOUGHT OF THIS.

THIS IS ON OUR BUCKET LIST BECAUSE:

_____

_____

_____

PLANS AND PREPARATIONS TO MAKE THIS HAPPEN:

_____

_____

_____

WE DID IT!

WHEN? _____ WHERE? _____

THE STORY OF OUR ADVENTURE:

_____

_____

_____

_____

_____

HIS BEST MEMORY: ( )

_____

HIS BEST MEMORY: ( )

_____

_____

.... THOUGHT OF THIS.

THIS IS ON OUR BUCKET LIST BECAUSE:

....

....

....

PLANS AND PREPARATIONS TO MAKE THIS HAPPEN:

....

....

....

WE DID IT!

WHEN? .... WHERE? ....

THE STORY OF OUR ADVENTURE:

....

....

....

....

....

HIS BEST MEMORY: ( )

....

HIS BEST MEMORY: ( )

....

....

ADVENTURE
#25:

.... THOUGHT OF THIS.

THIS IS ON OUR BUCKET LIST BECAUSE:

....

....

....

PLANS AND PREPARATIONS TO MAKE THIS HAPPEN:

....

....

....

WE DID IT!

WHEN? .... WHERE? ....

THE STORY OF OUR ADVENTURE:

....

....

....

....

....

HIS BEST MEMORY: ( )

....

HIS BEST MEMORY: ( )

....

....

ADVENTURE
#26:

.... THOUGHT OF THIS.

THIS IS ON OUR BUCKET LIST BECAUSE:

....

....

....

PLANS AND PREPARATIONS TO MAKE THIS HAPPEN:

....

....

....

WE DID IT!

WHEN? .... WHERE? ....

THE STORY OF OUR ADVENTURE:

....

....

....

....

....

HIS BEST MEMORY: (   )

....

HIS BEST MEMORY: (   )

....

ADVENTURE
27:

_____ THOUGHT OF THIS.

THIS IS ON OUR BUCKET LIST BECAUSE:

_____
_____
_____

PLANS AND PREPARATIONS TO MAKE THIS HAPPEN:

_____
_____
_____

WE DID IT!

WHEN? _____ WHERE? _____

THE STORY OF OUR ADVENTURE:

_____
_____
_____
_____
_____

HIS BEST MEMORY: ( )

_____

HIS BEST MEMORY: ( )

_____
_____

ADVENTURE
28:

_____ THOUGHT OF THIS.

THIS IS ON OUR BUCKET LIST BECAUSE:

_____

_____

_____

PLANS AND PREPARATIONS TO MAKE THIS HAPPEN:

_____

_____

_____

================ WE DID IT! ================

WHEN? _____ WHERE? _____

THE STORY OF OUR ADVENTURE:

_____

_____

_____

_____

_____

HIS BEST MEMORY: (   )

_____

HIS BEST MEMORY: (   )

_____

ADVENTURE
29:

.... THOUGHT OF THIS.

THIS IS ON OUR BUCKET LIST BECAUSE:

....
....
....

PLANS AND PREPARATIONS TO MAKE THIS HAPPEN:

....
....
....

WE DID IT!

WHEN? .... WHERE? ....

THE STORY OF OUR ADVENTURE:

....
....
....
....
....

HIS BEST MEMORY: ( )

....

HIS BEST MEMORY: ( )

....
....

ADVENTURE #30:

_____ THOUGHT OF THIS.

THIS IS ON OUR BUCKET LIST BECAUSE:

PLANS AND PREPARATIONS TO MAKE THIS HAPPEN:

WE DID IT!

WHEN? _____ WHERE? _____

THE STORY OF OUR ADVENTURE:

HIS BEST MEMORY: ( )

HIS BEST MEMORY: ( )

ADVENTURE
31:

_____ THOUGHT OF THIS.

THIS IS ON OUR BUCKET LIST BECAUSE:

_____

_____

_____

PLANS AND PREPARATIONS TO MAKE THIS HAPPEN:

_____

_____

_____

WE DID IT!

WHEN? _____ WHERE? _____

THE STORY OF OUR ADVENTURE:

_____

_____

_____

_____

_____

HIS BEST MEMORY: (   )

_____

HIS BEST MEMORY: (   )

_____

_____

ADVENTURE
32:

_____ THOUGHT OF THIS.

THIS IS ON OUR BUCKET LIST BECAUSE:

PLANS AND PREPARATIONS TO MAKE THIS HAPPEN:

WE DID IT!

WHEN? _____   WHERE? _____

THE STORY OF OUR ADVENTURE:

HIS BEST MEMORY: (   )

HIS BEST MEMORY: (   )

ADVENTURE
33:

_____ THOUGHT OF THIS.

THIS IS ON OUR BUCKET LIST BECAUSE:

_____
_____
_____

PLANS AND PREPARATIONS TO MAKE THIS HAPPEN:

_____
_____
_____

WE DID IT!

WHEN? _____ WHERE? _____

THE STORY OF OUR ADVENTURE:

_____
_____
_____
_____
_____

HIS BEST MEMORY: ( )

_____

HIS BEST MEMORY: ( )

_____

ADVENTURE
#34:

.... THOUGHT OF THIS.

THIS IS ON OUR BUCKET LIST BECAUSE:

PLANS AND PREPARATIONS TO MAKE THIS HAPPEN:

WE DID IT!

WHEN? .... WHERE? ....

THE STORY OF OUR ADVENTURE:

HIS BEST MEMORY: ( )

HIS BEST MEMORY: ( )

ADVENTURE
35:

_____ THOUGHT OF THIS.

THIS IS ON OUR BUCKET LIST BECAUSE:

_____

_____

_____

PLANS AND PREPARATIONS TO MAKE THIS HAPPEN:

_____

_____

_____

WE DID IT!

WHEN? _____ WHERE? _____

THE STORY OF OUR ADVENTURE:

_____

_____

_____

_____

_____

HIS BEST MEMORY: (   )

_____

HIS BEST MEMORY: (   )

_____

_____ THOUGHT OF THIS.

THIS IS ON OUR BUCKET LIST BECAUSE:

_____

_____

_____

PLANS AND PREPARATIONS TO MAKE THIS HAPPEN:

_____

_____

_____

WE DID IT!

WHEN? _____ WHERE? _____

THE STORY OF OUR ADVENTURE:

_____

_____

_____

_____

_____

HIS BEST MEMORY: ( )

_____

HIS BEST MEMORY: ( )

_____

_____

ADVENTURE
#37:

_____ THOUGHT OF THIS.

THIS IS ON OUR BUCKET LIST BECAUSE:

PLANS AND PREPARATIONS TO MAKE THIS HAPPEN:

WE DID IT!

WHEN? _____ WHERE? _____

THE STORY OF OUR ADVENTURE:

HIS BEST MEMORY: ( )

HIS BEST MEMORY: ( )

_____ THOUGHT OF THIS.

THIS IS ON OUR BUCKET LIST BECAUSE:

PLANS AND PREPARATIONS TO MAKE THIS HAPPEN:

WE DID IT!

WHEN? _____ WHERE? _____

THE STORY OF OUR ADVENTURE:

HIS BEST MEMORY: (   )

HIS BEST MEMORY: (   )

#39:

_____ THOUGHT OF THIS.

THIS IS ON OUR BUCKET LIST BECAUSE:

_____

_____

_____

PLANS AND PREPARATIONS TO MAKE THIS HAPPEN:

_____

_____

_____

WE DID IT!

WHEN? _____ WHERE? _____

THE STORY OF OUR ADVENTURE:

_____

_____

_____

_____

_____

HIS BEST MEMORY: (   )

_____

HIS BEST MEMORY: (   )

_____

ADVENTURE
#40:

_____ THOUGHT OF THIS.

THIS IS ON OUR BUCKET LIST BECAUSE:

_____

_____

_____

PLANS AND PREPARATIONS TO MAKE THIS HAPPEN:

_____

_____

_____

WE DID IT!

WHEN? _____ WHERE? _____

THE STORY OF OUR ADVENTURE:

_____

_____

_____

_____

_____

HIS BEST MEMORY: (   )

_____

HIS BEST MEMORY: (   )

_____

_____

ADVENTURE
41:

.... THOUGHT OF THIS.

THIS IS ON OUR BUCKET LIST BECAUSE:

PLANS AND PREPARATIONS TO MAKE THIS HAPPEN:

════════════════ WE DID IT! ════════════════

WHEN? .... WHERE? ....

THE STORY OF OUR ADVENTURE:

HIS BEST MEMORY: ( )

HIS BEST MEMORY: ( )

ADVENTURE
42:

_____ THOUGHT OF THIS.

THIS IS ON OUR BUCKET LIST BECAUSE:

PLANS AND PREPARATIONS TO MAKE THIS HAPPEN:

═══════════════ WE DID IT! ═══════════════

WHEN? _____ WHERE? _____

THE STORY OF OUR ADVENTURE:

HIS BEST MEMORY: (   )

HIS BEST MEMORY: (   )

_____ THOUGHT OF THIS.

THIS IS ON OUR BUCKET LIST BECAUSE:

_____

_____

_____

PLANS AND PREPARATIONS TO MAKE THIS HAPPEN:

_____

_____

_____

WE DID IT!

WHEN? _____ WHERE? _____

THE STORY OF OUR ADVENTURE:

_____

_____

_____

_____

_____

HIS BEST MEMORY: (   )

_____

HIS BEST MEMORY: (   )

_____

_____

ADVENTURE
44:

.... THOUGHT OF THIS.

THIS IS ON OUR BUCKET LIST BECAUSE:

PLANS AND PREPARATIONS TO MAKE THIS HAPPEN:

WE DID IT!

WHEN? .... WHERE? ....

THE STORY OF OUR ADVENTURE:

HIS BEST MEMORY: ( )

HIS BEST MEMORY: ( )

ADVENTURE
45:

.... THOUGHT OF THIS.

THIS IS ON OUR BUCKET LIST BECAUSE:

PLANS AND PREPARATIONS TO MAKE THIS HAPPEN:

═══════════════ WE DID IT! ═══════════════

WHEN? .... WHERE? ....

THE STORY OF OUR ADVENTURE:

HIS BEST MEMORY: ( )

HIS BEST MEMORY: ( )

ADVENTURE

#46:

_____ THOUGHT OF THIS.

THIS IS ON OUR BUCKET LIST BECAUSE:

_____

_____

_____

PLANS AND PREPARATIONS TO MAKE THIS HAPPEN:

_____

_____

_____

WE DID IT!

WHEN? _____ WHERE? _____

THE STORY OF OUR ADVENTURE:

_____

_____

_____

_____

_____

HIS BEST MEMORY: (   )

_____

HIS BEST MEMORY: (   )

_____

_____

ADVENTURE
47:

_____ THOUGHT OF THIS.

THIS IS ON OUR BUCKET LIST BECAUSE:

_____

_____

_____

PLANS AND PREPARATIONS TO MAKE THIS HAPPEN:

_____

_____

_____

WE DID IT!

WHEN? _____ WHERE? _____

THE STORY OF OUR ADVENTURE:

_____

_____

_____

_____

_____

HIS BEST MEMORY: ( )

_____

HIS BEST MEMORY: ( )

_____

ADVENTURE
48:

_____ THOUGHT OF THIS.

THIS IS ON OUR BUCKET LIST BECAUSE:

_____

_____

_____

PLANS AND PREPARATIONS TO MAKE THIS HAPPEN:

_____

_____

_____

WE DID IT!

WHEN? _____ WHERE? _____

THE STORY OF OUR ADVENTURE:

_____

_____

_____

_____

_____

HIS BEST MEMORY: (   )

_____

HIS BEST MEMORY: (   )

_____

_____

ADVENTURE
49:

.... THOUGHT OF THIS.

THIS IS ON OUR BUCKET LIST BECAUSE:

PLANS AND PREPARATIONS TO MAKE THIS HAPPEN:

WE DID IT!

WHEN? .... WHERE? ....

THE STORY OF OUR ADVENTURE:

HIS BEST MEMORY: ( )

HIS BEST MEMORY: ( )

ADVENTURE
#50:

.... THOUGHT OF THIS.

THIS IS ON OUR BUCKET LIST BECAUSE:

....

....

....

PLANS AND PREPARATIONS TO MAKE THIS HAPPEN:

....

....

....

WE DID IT!

WHEN? .... WHERE? ....

THE STORY OF OUR ADVENTURE:

....

....

....

....

....

HIS BEST MEMORY: (   )

....

HIS BEST MEMORY: (   )

....

....

ADVENTURE
#51:

_____ THOUGHT OF THIS.

THIS IS ON OUR BUCKET LIST BECAUSE:

....

....

....

PLANS AND PREPARATIONS TO MAKE THIS HAPPEN:

....

....

....

═══════════ WE DID IT! ═══════════

WHEN? _____   WHERE? _____

THE STORY OF OUR ADVENTURE:

....

....

....

....

....

HIS BEST MEMORY: (   )

....

HIS BEST MEMORY: (   )

....

ADVENTURE
52:
_____ THOUGHT OF THIS.

THIS IS ON OUR BUCKET LIST BECAUSE:
_____
_____
_____
_____

PLANS AND PREPARATIONS TO MAKE THIS HAPPEN:
_____
_____
_____
_____

WE DID IT!

WHEN? _____ WHERE? _____

THE STORY OF OUR ADVENTURE:
_____
_____
_____
_____
_____

HIS BEST MEMORY: (   )
_____

HIS BEST MEMORY: (   )
_____
_____

Printed in Great Britain
by Amazon